From Bitchy To Bitchin'

13 Tips To Be Happy Now!

Includes Journal

Vicky Ford

Longest Dedication Ever!

I would like to dedicate this book to
a whole bunch of people.

First of all, to my husband, Jim:

Thank you for your support and encouragement, your love and making married life so fun. I Love You.

To my children and grandchildren.
You inspire me every day in so many fun and unexpected ways.

To my family and friends;
Thank you for your words of encouragement and constantly asking, "When is your book done?" It meant I actually had to finish it instead of just talking about it.

And finally, to Mrs. McIntosh, the wonderful librarian at Vanderhoof Elementary School, throughout my grade school years.

Mrs. Lillian McIntosh gave me my love of books beginning when I was 7 and encouraged me in later years to continue my writing. She passed quietly in 2012, in bed, reading glasses on and an open book on her chest.

Thank you all.

Give
Every Day
The Chance
To Be The Most
Beautiful
Of Your
Life

Mark Twain

Table Of Contents

Kindness Begins With The Understanding That We All Struggle

Charles Glassman

Great Things
Never
Came
From
Comfort
Zones

- Introduction -

From Bitchy to Bitchin'
13 Tips To Be Happy Now

I began this book so many years ago that it is hard to remember when it hasn't been a part of my life.   I remember sitting on my small wicker love seat, the warmth of the spring sun soothing away the winter.

As my mind wandered through the twists and turns of my life I recalled the times I had experienced the "dark night of the soul" where, despite the love and caring of family and friends, I felt like hell.

But those darkest moments became turning points, where I *chose* the journey back to joy and happiness. I knew in my soul that my being happy or being miserable was a conscious choice or decision that was mine alone.   I am responsible for my own state of being.

As I put pen to paper the words simply wrote themselves.   I remember the feeling of empowerment that flowed through me.   I wanted to pass the essence of that on to others so they, too, would be inspired to take charge of their own lives and happiness.

And so, **From Bitchy to Bitchin'– 13 Tips To Be Happy Now**, came to be.

Along the way, I discovered what made me truly happy. I realized it really didn't have to be big, extravagant things, although a trip to somewhere warm and beachy makes me really happy.

I discovered great happiness in feeling the sun and wind on my face no matter where I am or blowing bubbles or enjoying hugs from my husband, family & friends.

I also found happiness in looking back at where I came from, taking the things I had learned, either from good or bad experiences, and building on those.

I loved creating affirmations as little reminders I could give myself throughout my day to stay positive, to focus on what I could do, could change, could create.

I came to know myself so much better in the process and in knowing my 'self' I came to love, accept and honor myself.

This book is for you. Through these pages I hope you come to know your own 'self' better, to see the world through new eyes, to know *you* are the Creator of your life. You deserve to be happy. You are worthy of having joy fill your life and soul.

So have fun on your own journey from Bitchy to Bitchin'.

Vicky M Ford

It's OK
If The
Only Thing
You Did
Today
Was Breathe

I Wish I Was
A Little Kid Again
So I Could
Take A Long Nap
And Everyone
Would Be Proud Of Me
Just for
Doing That

A World Full of Your Favourite Things

"Life is short and unpredictable.
Feed your soul by doing things that make you happy"
- Vicky Ford

Make a list of all your favorite things. I won't ask you to analyze the things on the list to see if it shows any weird personality traits. We all have those! And don't think too hard about it, either. This is fun! Today you are Oprah and the world is full of your favorite things!

Just let your mind wander. Think about your senses. What smells do you love? What about music? Did you ever think about what your favorite weather might be?

This is so much fun to do with your kids, too. They are very aware of sensations and their senses. It is all so new to them.

Here are a few of my favorite things in life.

- the feel of the wind as it blows across my face and through my hair.

- jeans with stretch in them. Best invention ever!

- reading a great fantasy adventure book.

- cooking up a meal to some awesome rock music

- Everything about horses. The feeling of connection and freedom when I fly across the open fields riding bareback, their intelligence. And yes, even their smell.

- Muppets Christmas Carol movie. This is one of my favorite movies ever. It is touching and funny, with great characters, wonderful songs and a performance by Michael Caine as the best Scrooge, ever

- having parties and gatherings with friends and family . We will have a party to celebrate just about anything; a renovated bathroom, because it's spring, New Years, or just because it's time to get everyone back together again

- occasionally sipping a really good tequila. Some tequilas are just meant to be savored, not shot. We like 1800 & Jimador Gold at the moment, after going through a Patron phase. It's smooth, light and hardly any bite. Thank you, Jutta, for introducing us to Jimador.

- the incredible feeling of connection and expansiveness I get during my meditations

- Kauai – I love the feeling I get when I land in Lihue and start heading through Kapa'a to Hanalei. I feel as though I am being welcomed home as soon as I put my feet in the water; that the grandmother spirit of Kauai has wrapped me in her arms and filled me with Aloha.

- swimming with the Manta Rays and dolphins off our friends boat in Kona. Just a magical experience. Check out Sunlight On Water for their tours.

- Travel to anywhere:

- Egypt was incredible; beyond what we could have imagined. You just have to go; there are no words.

- The Caribbean, with its history, music, art and people; turquoise water washing up against beaches of powder soft sand.

- New York was surreal and amazing. It was like stepping into a movie scene with the jackhammers going, the yellow cabs, fantastic people, cool old water towers on the rooftops, Broadway, Times Square, intricately designed vintage manhole covers. I Love New York.

- Australia has a beat all it's own. The people are great; they really do say "No worries." Love it! I loved the song birds, the beaches, the food.....the whole Aussie vibe was fun.

And I Love Nature

- white water rafting. A wet, wild, wonderful rush.

- hugs from grandkids. Just pure love

- the warmth of the sun on my body; especially if I am on a beach somewhere and can hear the ocean.

- the magical landscape after a snowfall. Imagine marshmallow fluff flung everywhere. It clings to every blade of grass, every tree branch and twig, every telephone wire. Everything is clean and pristine. Even the air has a softness to it.

- being in love. Isn't it great to be in love? The most important person to love is YOU.

- a coffee and Bailey's while sitting by the fire on a cold winter night.

- writing. I write about everything and it's something I love to share. Everyone has a story to tell. I love to write kid stories. They are so much fun and my kids and grandkids provide lots of material and ideas. It's a great way to just let your imagination fly freely.

- taking walks in the fall when all the Aspen trees are golden. September and October here is so beautiful. The Aspen trees really do look like they are filled with shiny, golden coins. When the wind comes up you are just surrounded by swirling color; the forest pathways become Dorothy's Yellow Brick Road.

- curling up on a cold, rainy Sunday afternoon to watch a movie with my hubby and grandkids.

-   our hot tub.   I couldn't make it through a winter without that hot tub. On winter nights, warm and protected from the cold, we can sit out under the most incredible skyscape.   We watched an entire full lunar eclipse one night and many meteor showers shooting fireworks in every direction.

-   We have watched the sun come up, firing red, purple and orange light across the sky like a 60's light show.   We play water games with the grandkids, we've watched deer, moose and bear wander through the yard and I've even used it to do some water aerobics.

-   sunsets from our cabin at the lake.   Just Wow!

-   cooking with sisters, daughters, friends, grandkids. This is so much fun. One Christmas we had 7 of us cooking dinner; Margaritas in one hand, sharp knife in the other. Just kidding.

OK, now it's your turn.

This week, as you think of all the things in your life that you love, what starts to happen? Your heart space opens up. You begin to recognize the many things in your own life that are precious and good. Nurture this heart space; be aware of how there are so many things, even small things, to be grateful for.

How has making this list changed your perspective about your own life?

A World Full Of Your Favorite Things

Have fun writing down a few of your favorite things.
Everything goes on the list, from seeing the first butterfly in Spring to having the perfect wedding day.

Why Be
Moody
When You Can
Shake
Your Booty

Life
Is
Better
When
You're
Laughing

How Does Your Garden Grow?

"The glory of gardening: hands in the dirt, head in the sun, heart with nature. To nurture a garden is to feed not just the body, but the soul."

- Alfred Austin

Listen to Alfred. Feed your soul; plant a garden. It doesn't have to be big; indeed there are so many apartment dwellers that pots on a balcony will do.

There is such a satisfaction in planting the seeds, tending them and then being rewarded with lettuce for your salad or flowers for your table.

It doesn't have to be a big garden. I have planted potatoes in whisky barrels and gotten a good crop. Just a few seeds in a planter box will do.

Herbs, like thyme and oregano, are very easy to grow and hardy as well. Some people like to buy tomato or pepper plants to set out on the deck and they look beautiful. Once your start looking at the wonderful variety of seed available you will have a hard time stopping at just a few.

A mix of rainbow chard and assorted lettuces will look fantastic in a planter box. Plant a mix of green, yellow and purple beans that will look like art in a plain, round pot.

Look at flowers like Gazania, Snapdragons, Pansies, Petunias and Nasturtiums as easy to grow options. Geraniums and Million bells are really great together as well.

Soon you will be color coordinating and companion planting with the best of them and your green thumb will begin to show itself.

Think back to when you were a kid. For some of us it just felt so good to get our hands in the dirt. I made mud pies decorated with flowers, villages in the sand box with roads for cars.

In the fall us kids helped my Mom and Dad dig up potatoes and carrots in the fall.

Growing and nurturing plants, whether they are in a purple pot on your windowsill or in a garden big enough to feed half the neighborhood, is intensely satisfying.

And it's a wonderful way to connect to the earth as well, even if you are gardening on the twentieth floor.

Having green, growing plants in your environment has the same calming, soothing effect that being in nature provides; good for the soul.

What types of plants did you choose for your balcony garden?

How does it feel to be growing your own veggies?

Does having a little balcony oasis change the way your space feels?

Over the next week bring some greenery into your home and watch your happiness quotient rise.

How Does Your Garden Grow?

There is something so satisfying about
nurturing plants and working with
Mother Earth.
Let your imagination go and whether you
have one pot on a balcony or have acres
to play with, just enjoy the journey.

You Don't Have To Be
Good At
Gardening
For
Gardening
To Be Good For You

Life's A
Garden.
Dig It

The Gift of Friendship

*"In everybody's life, at some time, our inner fire goes out.
It is then burst into flame by an encounter with another
human being. We should all be thankful for those
people who rekindle the inner spirit."*
- Albert Schweitzer

Where would we be without our friends? They pick us up when we are down, they love us when we are cranky and they laugh with us through life.

So why did those incredible people in your life choose you to be their friend? What qualities did they find in you that made them stick around after they had seen you at your worst?

Not many people actually know why they are chosen to be someone's friend.

This is such a wonderful thing to do. Your friends will show you a vision of yourself that, many times, you don't see for yourself. When you discover your best qualities through their eyes, you will come to know and value those things even more.

I think there is value in seeing yourself through another's eyes. We don't always recognize our amazing qualities and traits. And our friends will be straight with us, too.

And if you are going to ask your friends what your friendship means to them, it's a wonderful treat to have your list of reasons prepared as to why you have chosen them as friends. They will ask, you know.

Don't save this stuff for the funeral. Share with them now how much you value their friendship and the things that make them such an important part of your life.

Wasn't it great to share all that great stuff with each other?

What did you learn about yourself?

Was there a quality that more than one person felt was important and wonderful about you?

Who else can you do this with? - Mom, Dad, sisters, brothers, other friends and neighbors, the grocery cashier. There are so many people that touch our lives and this is a beautiful way to let them know just how much they mean to us.

This is a simple yet powerful gift that you can share today, during the coming week and throughout your life.

The Gift Of Friendship

Use this space to write down a few things
that make your friends so special.
Then share it with them
Trust me, they will really love it!

A True Friendship
Is Based
On A Combination Of
Laughter,
Inappropriateness,
Shenanigans
&
At Times...Wine

I walked along the busy street,
and as far as I could see,
Angels went about their day.
They looked like you and me.
~ Vicky M. Ford

Be Someone's Angel Today

"Real generosity is doing something kind for someone who will never find out."
- Frank A. Clark

Frank Clark wrote brilliant, thoughtful one-liners for a daily feature in the Des Moines Tribune called "The Country Parson" from 1955 till sometime in the 1980's. He passed in 1991 at 80 years young.

He was quoted once as saying that "most of the good things that happened to me in my career, happened to me when I was trying to help someone else."

Today is the perfect day to do something nice for someone without them finding out "who dunnit."

It could be as simple as putting money in someone's expired meter or giving a flower to a stranger who will never know your name.

A simple kindness has the wonderful potential to change a life.

Leo Buscaglia once said

"Too often we underestimate the power of a touch, a smile, a kind word, a listening ear, an honest compliment, or the smallest act of caring, all of which have the potential to turn a life around."

There are many stories that tell of a person on the brink of desperate action, whose life has been changed by the simplest kindness from a stranger.

Being someone's Angel doesn't mean doing good on the "Oprah Scale." Your smile, your kind words, a hug or buying an extra lunch to give are as important.

You might donate gift cards for a grocery store to an organization that helps single parents.

It's easy to leave a nice note on someone's windshield, pay for someone's lunch tab on your way out of the restaurant or send a small gift to someone who is experiencing challenges.

I think it would be so fun to buy flowers and just hand them out to folks on the street.

It's one of the most wonderful feelings simply to know you have made a difference in someone's life, made them smile or helped them remember that the world truly is a wonderful place and there are good people.

The important thing to remember is this: You may never know what your Angelic Act meant to another. And that's OK.

I remember one particularly rotten day years ago. Our daughter had just had surgery and we were waiting to hear if there was cancer in her lymph nodes. I was sick with fear and worry.

We had her young daughter with us so she could visit and then received more troubling news about a whole different situation. I found out that day what the word 'overwrought' meant.

My sister had driven me downtown and as I walked up to the door of the liquor store…..yes, I needed a drink… a young man opened it for me and as I walked past he said "You look really beautiful today."

Well, at first I thought he was talking to someone else. But he was looking at me!! So then I thought "he must need glasses cuz I know I look like hell."

But he smiled at me as I stammered Thank You. I almost cried. Suddenly the load wasn't so heavy. I got back in my sister's car and told her all about this wonderful man and then she said, "I didn't see anyone go in there with you." Cue mysterious music.

And to top it off, my lovely sister gave me a gorgeous coat I had once complimented her on.

Angels truly are everywhere and they look like you and me. I've even read incredible stories of people who have been saved by all sorts of animals.

Folks have been rescued in the forest and at sea by the creatures who live there. And we've all heard of cats, dogs, birds, horses, who have saved humans from disaster.

There are many stories that tell of a person on the brink of desperate action, whose life has been changed by the simplest kindness from a stranger.

Let that stranger be you today. Be someone's Angel this week.

Does the thought of being someone's Angel make you smile?

How many things can you think of that you can do today to make someone's day just a little bit better?

In the past, has someone's kind word or smile helped brighten your day?

Be Someone's Angel Today

Being someone's Angel is fun,
easy and makes you feel so great!
What were your favorite Angel Actions?

Your Wings
Already Exist.
All You Have To Do
Is
FLY

I Could Not
Have Made It
This Far
Had There Not
Been Angels
Along The Way

Della Reese
Actress

Good Reads for Your Spiritual Journey

"The things I want to know are in books.; my best friend is the man who'll get me a book I ain't read."
- Abraham Lincoln

I have been book crazy ever since I can remember. I was the kid in school with the Math book propped up on the desk and the trashy novel hidden inside. I guess that could be why I got D's in Math but A in English.

When I worked in the local mall I would buy beautiful cookbooks to read on my lunch hour. Even now, a browse through a great cookbook with beautiful pictures will lift my spirits. It inspires me to reach new heights in the kitchen......if I ever get around to it. Tomorrow's looking good.

Our favorite books for summer reading at the cabin include all the Calvin and Hobbes books. Through Calvin we live the frustrations we grownups sometimes feel at life.

We live vicariously through Calvin and his buddy, Hobbes as they play Calvinball....making up the rules as they go along, adding changes on a whim. Don't you wish your life was sometimes like that? I don't like the way this is going; *new rules*!

At times I immerse myself in a fantastic Terry Pratchett novel, and I can easily become part of one of the wild, crazy worlds that he has created.

It's a world where Death can take a vacation while his pet rat takes over; where the Head Librarian at the University is an Orangutan and where the magical spells of Rincewind the Magician, backfire more often than not. Much like my life sometimes.

I have read so many books on spirituality that I have lost count and even if I did not agree with everything the author had written I always received the exact thing I needed most at the time.

More than simply being a way to pass the time, the books I have read have helped me discover things about myself I could not know. They have given me ideas to ponder, concepts that have stretched my beliefs and ideas of what is possible.

I have come to enjoy and relish a book that causes me to think the impossible, possible.

My books are also a wonderful source of inspiration, guidance and awakening. The writers give me hints about who I am as a spiritual being and then let me come to my own conclusions. They open the door and I choose whether or not to step through.

Here are some of my favorite books. Some are older but no less fun, relevant and inspiring.

Anything by Terry Pratchett. Weird & wonderful.
The Hobbit & Lord of the Rings – J.R.R. Tolkien
The Celestine Prophecy Series – James Redfield
The Biology of Belief – Dr. Bruce Lipton
Remember – Steve Rother
Wishcraft – Barbara Sheer
Q.   The Autobiography of Quincy Jones
The Red Pyramid Series – Rick Riordan
The Mists Of Avalon – Marion Zimmer Bradley
The Kon-Tiki – Thor Heyerdahl
The Ten Levels Of DNA – Lee Carroll – Kryon Series
Harry Potter – J. K. Rowling
Eragon Series – Christopher Paolini
The Tao of Pooh - Benjamin Hoff
Doreen Virtue's Angel Books
Writing Down The Bones – Natalie Goldberg
Any Books by Gregg Braden
Grass Beyond The Mountains Series – Rich Hobson
Any Books by Bernie Siegel
Books About Miracles, Angels, Magic, Love
Chicken Soup For The Soul Books
Grandpere – A terrific book that teaches us how to step into life's changes as a natural part of being human by my dear friend, Janet Romain
Books by Wayne Dyer
Books by Louise Hay and Cheryl Richardson
Autobiography of a Yogi – Paramahansa Yogananda
Books by Kahlil Gibran
Tuesdays With Morrie – Mitch Albom
Books by Richard Carlson – Don't Sweat The Small Stuff

This is by no means a complete list. I may discover an old castoff book at a yard sale that seems as though it was written for me. Or sometimes a book will just fall off the shelf at the bookstore and land at my feet. Well you know I have to read that one!

There are as many books out there as there are folks with a message to share. Go ahead. Explore many different view points and perspectives, take what rings true for you and leave the rest.

I love books that make me feel good at the end, make me think, make me laugh; make me want to be a better person.

What types of books just make you feel good when you read them? Are there any authors that hit the mark with what you need to know at the time? It's almost as though they are writing for you.

If you are not into a whole, great big book, start with anthologies. There are so many kinds out there, starting with Chicken Soup For The Soul. They are filled with short stories that will uplift you, give you strength and hope, make you laugh, make you cry and maybe change the path you are on right now.

This week read one thing that makes you think or laugh or cry or just say "Wow, that was cool."

Good Reads For Your Spiritual Journey

What are some of the inspirational books that have helped you in your journey?

Sometimes
You Just Need To
Lay On The
Couch
And Read
For A Couple Of Years

Reading
Forces You To Be
Quiet
In A World
That No Longer
Makes A Place
For That

John Green

Art Therapy – Good for the Soul

"The purpose of art is washing the dust of daily life off our souls."

\- Pablo Picasso

Need a little pick-me-up? Go picture shopping. In my world, art is therapy.

Even if there are no blank spaces on your wall at the moment, if your heart races just a little when you see a piece of art, then maybe it should come home with you. Just make sure you don't break the bank.

It needn't be big or expensive and can even be something that no one but you and the artist understands. A single art piece can bring the energy of your space to a whole new happy place.

I believe art has an important place in our lives and in our world. Art gives us a unique way of expressing our individual perception of life yet brings us together. It makes us think, it inspires us, it gives us pleasure and enjoyment, sometimes it puzzles or confuses us.

The art pieces we choose to have in our homes are a reflection of ourselves.   In our own home we have several great paintings by a friend who is so talented and imaginative. She once told me that when she "senses' at painting in her mind, it HAS to come out onto the canvas..

One   is the face of a First Nations woman but all the details have been created by integrating the faces of all the cultures of the world within it. It brings home to me that all the peoples of the world are a very diverse family.

The other is the face of a wonderful old, wizardy man with windswept white hair and beard and compelling eyes. I love it!

We have another piece that is a seriolithograph created and signed by actor Anthony Quinn. It is of a Bedouin man; his face, so serene, and his eyes have just an endless depth.   My husband and I purchased it in Hawai'i in the 1980's after much "discussion."

It is now worth more than 5 times what we paid for it. But even if it had cost $15.00 as a poster, it doesn't matter. The price has nothing to do with how I feel about this treasure.   I am still so in love with this painting.   I feel peaceful whenever I look at it and it brings a sense of calm to my home.   His eyes show endless dimension and possibilities.

Another favorite is a wonderful sepia toned movie poster remake from the 1949 movie She Wore A Yellow Ribbon, with John Wayne. It is a great piece of history. We have a print of a young man named Terry Fox. After having lost a leg to cancer he chose to train for a run across Canada. He made it about half way before the cancer returned. He died at the age of 23. I am inspired and encouraged by his strength.

Three other art pieces are pictures I found in magazines and had framed. One is a really cool blue strawberry. The other two are of wild jungle cats and for the cost of a frame, I have a pieces of art that I will never get tired of.

What kind of artwork touches you? Is it ocean scenes or wildlife, cubism or expressionist, steampunk or Renoir?

What thoughts or feelings does your favorite artwork bring out in you?

Does the work of Michelangelo inspire feelings of awe at the incredible detail and vision? His variety of subject matter is a testament to his curiosity and ability to look at the world from a place of expanded awareness.

Ocean scenes may bring you peace and calm while more contemporary artwork makes you feel more vibrant and alive through its wonderful use of color, shape and movement.

It's fun to experiment with different pieces with their unique use of color, technique, themes, movement and ideas. You are, in essence, looking into the soul of the artist.

There are many great places to search out your next piece of art and they have nothing to do with spending many thousands of dollars at Sothebys or Christies Auction houses.

I have framed greeting cards of every description as pieces of art in our house that I have picked up from card shops, drug stores, dollar stores and from friends and family.

I love cards because, no matter what your taste in art may be, there is something out there that will tickle your fancy. They are small enough to group them as one artistic display or pop one or two in little corners to give a little pop of color or fun in unexpected places.

There are also online poster shops, sites like Etsy and ebay, and artists on fiverr that can create a custom piece from anything your mind can come up with.

Using a smart phone and a graphics program or photo shop anyone can become an artist. You might take a picture of a bicycle wheel, crop it so one corner is showing then change the color to sepia or black and white and Voila! Ready made art. Search out a vintage frame from ebay or nearby thrift shop and you have a unique art piece that expresses you.

Perhaps it is your turn, this week, to become the artist. Don't be afraid to pick up the paintbrush or chisel, a chainsaw or knitting needle and give permanent expression to those visions that lie within your soul.

Art Therapy

What are some of your favorite forms of art?
What kind of art touches you?
What emotions, ideas, insights does your artwork inspire within you?

No
Artist
Tolerate
Reality

Nietzsche

Art
Is Chaos
Taking Shape

Picasso

Great Accomplishments, Large and Small

"Man is always more than he can know of himself; consequently, his accomplishments, time and again, will come as a surprise to him."
- Henry Wadsworth Longfellow

This is the ultimate 'You Rock' list.

It's a list of the things that you have accomplished in your time here on Earth.......so far.   You can include everything from your greatest accomplishments to the fact that you can tell time on an "old fashioned watch" with hands.

Each time you add something to your list, notice how it makes you feel. You will start to feel a little lighter, a little happier, a little better about being you.

Hell, you need to be excited about being YOU!!!

There is only one of you.   There will never, in the history of the world, be anyone quite like you. You are unique and amazing and, spectacular.

Own it, baby!

Here is a short list to get you started.

- Are you good at sports? Can you sink a basketball from 30 feet? Have you mastered the Hula Hoop? Did you finally make it through a Zumba class without collapsing? Did you complete the Iron Man Triathlon, beating your own best time or did you simply manage to jog around the block without stopping? Everything goes on the list, no matter how small.

- Are you a stay at home parent of toddlers who manages to keep your house clean? If so, how did you do it? I sure couldn't.

- Can you cook a great soup? Or just the best grilled cheese sandwich, ever!   Perhaps you throw the best dinner parties that have your friends lined up at the door for your food. Or, like my friend Janet, you make the best butter tarts in the world.

- Have you survived raising your kids to adulthood with your sanity intact?   If so, YOU should write a book.

- Are you a Power Tool Priestess?   Or a Car-Fixing Superhero? Heck, even if you have figured out how to put air in the tires or can tell the difference between a Philips, a French Recess and a Roberts screwdriver, write it down.

- Have you lost that first 5 pounds as you change your diet to one that is healthier for you?

- Can you sing without causing the neighborhood dogs to howl?

- Do people just like to be around you because you make them feel good? Do they call when they are blue because you know just the right things to say and they know you are someone who really cares?

- Do you give great hugs?

So you see, what we put down on our list doesn't have to be life changing, award winning, earth-shattering. Not everyone runs their own Fortune 500 Company. We can't all grow freakishly large vegetables and we don't all have the "perfect" body.

Write down everything you can think of from the very beginning. By the time you are done with that list, you should be feeling pretty good about what you have accomplished so far.   You are feeling braver, more competent and happier with your life and yourself.

Now, don't tuck that list away in the back of your underwear drawer. No, no.

Now that you are inspired, find a special book to keep your list in and keep it accessible for those "not so perky" days.

You may even start a journal book and just keep adding till you need Volume 2, 3, 4, 5....

Now it's your turn. Make the next seven days about you and all that you have done, big and small.

Pull out that blank journal you tucked away years ago after watching an Oprah show. Start now.

You will never stop doing great things.

Great Accomplishments, Large & Small

From the time you were born you've accomplished great things.
Now it's time to acknowledge them all, large & small.

Forgiveness
Is A Gift
You Give Yourself

The Art of Forgiveness

"I have learned, that the person I have to ask forgiveness from the most is: myself. You must love yourself.
You have to forgive yourself, every day, whenever you remember a shortcoming, a flaw; you have to tell yourself "That's just fine".
You have to forgive yourself so much, until you don't even see those things anymore. Because that's what love is like."

- c.joybell c.

Forgiveness is Love. Love is Forgiveness.

First and foremost love yourself enough to forgive yourself. So many people carry guilt and pain with them for past mistakes. And that is exactly what they are; mistakes.

It is from mistakes that we learn and grow. Mistakes carry with them a certain amount of pain and shame mixed in with some serious feelings of anger at oneself but from these low points in our lives comes great wisdom and knowledge.

Forgiving yourself is loving yourself. It is saying that, despite the fact that you screwed up, no matter how badly, you are still OK.

As you forgive yourself you will find that it will be easier to forgive others who you feel have wronged you.

Forgiving them does not mean that you condone their actions.

The act of forgiving them is not as much for their well being as it is for yours.

Harboring anger, resentment, hatred against another is like *you* taking the poison, expecting *them* to die. Those negative emotions are a toxin in your body and can take a toll on your physical and emotional health.

It is not just about taking the high road but about caring for yourself by releasing those toxic emotions. It is like cutting that person or situation free, only you are the one who gains the freedom.

There are many methods that can be of help to you in this process.

- Traditional therapy. This can come in many forms. Look into the different therapy modalities and find the one that feels it would suit you the best.

Remember that their actions towards you were really coming from a place of anguish within their own soul.

They were acting from their own personal level of consciousness using the only tools they felt they had in that situation.

- Create a sacred, loving space around you. You may ask for Angels, Christ, God, Buddha, your higher self, guides, animal totems or any other supportive energy you identify with to be with you.

Ask that person's higher self to be with you in that space where there is only love. From this space you are able to forgive them. This is not the physical self that caused your pain and suffering, it is the highest expression of their soul. Healing can begin from this space.

- Meditation is not only used for relaxation and contemplating your belly button. There are as many meditations as there are reasons to want to do one.

You can use YouTube and Google to find some really good meditations on forgiveness. There are sites that specialize in offering only meditations. Once you start you will love how you feel afterwards.

 - Surround yourself with loving energy. Within that space, write a letter to whomever you are either asking forgiveness from, including yourself, or wishing to forgive.

Pour out your heart. If it is someone you are trying to forgive, including yourself, let them know how their actions have affected your life. You don't have to relive everything they did, simply focus on how you have been affected.

As you write your words, imagine every negative emotion attaching to the words and leaving your body, your mind, your cells. Feel the lightness, freedom and space that is left by releasing those emotions onto the paper.

Create a special ceremony.   It doesn't have to be elaborate, although this process is signifying a big change in your life, so make it meaningful. Then light that letter on fire.

As you watch this letter go up in flames, feel the release within your body. Smile as you watch that pain dissolve into the fire and smoke. As the flames begin to die down - forgive.

If you are asking someone for forgiveness, as you write your letter, simply say how sorry you are, what you have learned and simply ask their forgiveness. Don't make excuses for your behavior; it doesn't serve any purpose.

If you are able, you may wish to visit this person and ask face to face.   If this is not possible or just too painful then use the same process as above and burn the letter.

If they are still living you may be surprised to get a phone call or email from them.

If they are not in the physical, don't be surprised if you have a happy dream about them soon after your ceremony.

- Ho'oponopono is a Hawaiian practice of forgiveness. It is also found in various forms throughout the South Pacific. Ho'o is translated as "to". Ponopono can be translated as "make right or set right".

Our lovely Hawaiian friend told me that in his family everyone would gather after dinner. They would start with their grievances and through discussion, prayer, restitution and forgiveness the matter was closed.

Afterward there would be a time for giving praise, congratulations, gratitude and accolades to everyone. It always ended the evening in a very positive manner. Forgiveness and releasing of grievances always came first.

The basic words to use in Ho'oponopono are;

I am sorry
Please forgive me
Thank you
I love you

For a wonderful story on how incredibly powerful Ho'oponopono can be, Google Dr. Hew Len. He truly created miracles in the prison where he worked.

- As humans we seem to have a natural tendency to accumulate negative baggage that simply weighs us down. Happily, there are also many ways to help us release it all and live happier lives.

1.   Theta Therapy – this is a technique where the practitioner takes you into theta brain wave and helps you to release negative emotions

2.   EFT – Emotional Field Therapy – uses a tapping motion on various body points that help in the release of negative emotions.

3. Emotion Code and Body Code – uses muscle testing and magnets to find and release beliefs and emotions that have become trapped in our bodies.   This technique was created by a chiropractor in the United States.

There are many more modalities that you will find that can assist you in releasing those trapped emotions of anger, grief, resentment and help you to forgive.

We are all on a quest to live our lives in a healthier, happier and more balanced way. If you find that you are reliving a traumatic situation over and over, you can be sure that those negative emotions are trapped within your body.

They may make show up in your body as headaches, sinus conditions, aching joints and muscles, immune conditions, cancer, depression and many others conditions.

Once the emotion has been released from your body, many times the condition will be released or show reduced intensity as well.

Once the emotion has been released from your body, many times the condition will be released or show reduced intensity as well.

How do you know whether you have an emotion or trauma trapped within your body? If you think of the situation and still feel that emotional charge, it is still there and needs to be taken care of.

You could call this 'Freedom Week'. Freedom from the burdens and guilt that have bogged you down and kept you from being your own true self.

Is there someone you need to forgive or would like to ask forgiveness from?

What would you say to them?

How do you feel about forgiving yourself for your own past mistakes?

After your release work, how do you feel about the situation or person now?

Has it made a difference in how you see other situations in your life?

Are you quicker to forgive now that you are in this different space?

Is it easier to see that, in order to truly love, one must forgive oneself first?

Once the emotion has been released from your body, many times the condition will be released or show reduced intensity as well.

How do you know whether you have an emotion or trauma trapped within your body? If you think of the situation and still feel that emotional charge, it is still there and needs to be taken care of.

You could call this 'Freedom Week'. Freedom from the burdens and guilt that have bogged you down and kept you from being your own true self.

Is there someone you need to forgive or would like to ask forgiveness from?

What would you say to them?

How do you feel about forgiving yourself for your own past mistakes?

After your release work, how do you feel about the situation or person now?

Has it made a difference in how you see other situations in your life?

Are you quicker to forgive now that you are in this different space?

Is it easier to see that, in order to truly love, one must forgive oneself first?

The Art Of Forgiveness

Create a short list of anyone you feel you
can forgive, including yourself.
Write down the action you wish to take.

Forgiveness Brings Peace

Setting Boundaries
Is As Easy As
Saying
No.

Examine What
You Tolerate.
Self Care
Is How You
Take Your
Power Back

It's All About Boundaries

"To free us from the expectations of others, to give us back to ourselves – there lies the great singular power of self- respect."

- Joan Didion

Yes, setting boundaries is all about self-respect. It is honoring who you are and having others respect that. It says, "This is OK. This is not OK."

You have chosen to live your life in this time and place because you have something to contribute to the evolution of humanity and the planet. You are a part of the solution.

In your marriage, in your community, in the workplace you deserve to be heard. Each and every one of us is capable of true inspiration and even downright brilliance at times. Let that shine. Honor yourself and your contributions. We each have our moments.

At work it is so important to set solid boundaries. When are you available? Do you accept calls after work hours?

The advent of technology means that work can now follow us anywhere. What boundaries are you creating now so work do not overlap into your playtime?

Of course, common sense must rule. If your job requires you to be on call for part of the time you are away from your workspace, you just might be looking for another job if you tell your boss "Sorry, I have my boundaries set now."

He may simply say, "Screw your boundaries." But if you explain to them that your family time is important to you and point out that you work your tail off while you are in the office, there can always be points where agreements and compromises can be made.

Setting boundaries is a very important part of self-care. A great idea is to have a routine for morning and evening. Take a few quiet moments and take a few deep breaths. Imagine the sun pouring light down through the top of your head, through your body and out your feet into the earth. Let it expand outward till you feel like a glowing sphere of light.

Throughout your day notice how you feel around certain people. Are there co-workers or friends that just seem to drain your energy or agitate you simply by being near? Is there someone in your life who is super critical of you, your lifestyle, your shape, your work habits and your bad hair day?

You *can* make a stand with these people in a firm but gracious way. Simply let them know that their comments or behavior is not acceptable to you, smile and walk away.

Or you could come at them with your arms outstretched saying, "Someone needs a hug!!"   That will have them on the run for sure.

I had a very close friend who, over the years, became more and more negative and morose. I felt as though she was sucking the life right out of me with her stories of horror and death, gossip and fear. If there was a happy story happening she could find the dark side.

I am a pretty good at conflict avoidance so it took everything I had finally tell her that either she keep the conversation positive or not to come over. To my surprise, she did try to change her negative outlook on life.

Instead of me not ever answering my phone again when she called or moving out of the country to avoid her, we have remained friends. I am so glad that I was able to enforce those boundaries and let her know what was acceptable to me.

In all relationships each person brings something special to it. When one person's outlook or opinions are not being respected it creates hurt feelings.   One partner feels unappreciated, unloved, frustrated and not heard.

The other person can feel that he or she has the tremendous burden of making all the decisions and may also feel unappreciated and frustrated.

Setting boundaries is all about communication. It is respecting yourself enough to let your opinions and voice be heard. You must know within what you will or will not stand for.

There will always be those who push the limits. Ultimately it is you who must decide when to say NO!

Honor yourself this week. Love yourself enough to set good, strong boundaries and set into motion skills and tools that will last you a lifetime.

Are there some areas in your life where you already know that boundaries need to be set by you?

What is holding you back?

What steps can you take now to create and enforce your boundaries? Can you say no to the next telemarketer?

Can you tell the next person that talks down to you, that you just can't hear them when they use that tone of voice?

If you were asked to take on extra duties at work, at home, at your children's school, can you be firm in saying "not at this time" in a firm and gracious manner?

This week look at areas where you feel disempowered. Make the decision to assert yourself and create boundaries that are good for you.

You will not believe how great it feels to stand up for yourself in even the smallest way. Yahoo You!!

The time for being a doormat is over and it's time for you to take your power.   We no longer live in an age where it is OK to give that power to someone else. It is essentially giving them control over our lives.

And I do understand that there are times when you have to choose to just 'suck it up."

Hell, we all do that. But if you begin to take steps now in setting boundaries you will be amazed at how differently you are treated.

When I told my friend that I did not want to have her negative attitude in my house, I risked losing a friend. But, happily, that is not the way it worked out.

Just take that risk.   Start small. But remember that you must value yourself, your time and your life. You are worth it!

It's All About Boundaries

List areas of your life where it's time to
create stronger boundaries.
What actions can you take today?

The Best Memories
Come From
The Worst Ideas
Done With
Best Friends

Friends – Our Most Profound Teachers

*"We'll be friends forever, won't we Pooh?' asked Piglet.
'Even longer,' Pooh answered."*
- A.A. Milne, Winnie-the-Pooh

We all have situations that challenge us.

It doesn't matter whether it is completing a climb in the Himalayas, or just smiling and saying hello to a stranger. Each can be daunting in its own way.

One of my challenges is that I have always been somewhat shy around people I don't know well. I find that, unless they start a conversation with me, I just can't seem to put two words together.

But after watching my good friend, Lynn, while in Hawai'i with her a few years ago, I knew that being a whole lot less shy was a gift I had to cultivate within myself.

Wherever she is, when she walks down the street she will always have a smile on her face and a positive comment for many she meets.

During one short walk we took in Honolulu she praised the workmanship of a man creating wood carvings, told a lovely elderly woman how beautiful she was, spoke a few Hawaiian words to a couple of young guys and got smiles and Alohas in return.

I am so grateful for these experiences with her. I saw how easy it could be and how, in this small but significant act of kindness and friendship, she is creating a happier, more joyful world.

I have released some of my own self-imposed fears and now look for opportunities to live more like my friend, Lynn. I refuse to let shyness keep me from giving a smile and a Hello or a sharing laughter with the people we met on the street.

I think this quote is a question we must each ask ourselves upon waking in the morning to start a new day.

"Tell me, what is it you plan to do with your one wild and precious life?"

- Mary Oliver -

And life is wild and precious. We only have a certain number of days on this earth and so many choices in how to spend them. It's up to us to make each day count, whether it is doing something huge and grand or whether it is sharing a hug with a grieving friend.

We are blessed to have so many amazing friends in our life. I would not be who I am today without their love, their support, their honesty, their laughter and great hugs.

We are blessed to have so many amazing friends in our life. I would not be who I am today without their love, their support, their honesty, their laughter and great hugs.

Each one is a gift. I learned about myself, both good and bad. They taught me about forgiveness, tolerance, self-acceptance, boundaries, how to be a better friend, and so much more.

Are there any areas of your life where you feel it's time to be a little more daring and wild?

What one small step can you make today to start living a life that is full to the brim with experiences, love, laughter, bravery, learning, and excitement?

Don't try and change your whole life at once. This week choose one area and try something new.

The toughest thing in the world is to move past your own fear or uncertainty and step out into the world to shine your own light.

But the world needs your special light so shine brightly!

Friends –
Our Most Wonderful Teachers

What fun things have your learned from
your friends?
Does this idea change the way you see
your friends?

If You Stumble,
Make It
Part Of The Dance

Dance
First.
Think
Later.
It's The Natural Order

Doing Your Happy Dance

"I, not events, have the power to make me happy or unhappy today. I have the power to choose which it shall be. Yesterday is dead, tomorrow hasn't arrived yet. I have just one day, today, and I am going to be happy in it."

- Groucho Marx

Did you know that your happiness in this life is solely your responsibility? I know. I can just hear you saying, "Well, that sucks."

Sure, it would be great if we could blame someone else for our crappy day. It certainly doesn't feel like it should be all our fault! Lord knows, you've tried and tried to make it all work but it's like juggling chainsaws sometimes.

The bad news is that we can't really be happy 100% of the time. There will be days when it feels like life just beats you up and leaves you for dead.

I remember one snowy night years ago. I heard my husband's truck pull into the driveway. About 10 minutes later he walks in and without a word, went and poured himself about 4 ounces of whiskey and drank it down.

"What the hell happened?" I asked.

Turns out, when he drove in the driveway, and as the headlights hit where the shop should be, all he saw was a roof about 5 feet off the ground.

There was so much snow on the top that when it started to slide off to the back, it shifted the whole roof with it and the whole building had caved in.

When we could finally take a look at the damage we found the boat had been squashed, shelves broken and windows smashed. We had to wait till spring thaw before we could do anything about it.

Thankfully, insurance paid for most of the damage but the poor boat still has fiberglass streaks on it making it look like a Frankenboat.

The good news is that we *can* change our state of mind.

Now, I am not sure how much the whiskey helped that night and that certainly is not the path to happiness, although I know many who have tried it.

It is about choosing your state of mind and shifting your attitude towards life. It is how *you* view life. It is your level of optimism that determines how happy you are.

Is your glass half empty or half full?

Does your cup runneth over or is there a hole in your Happy Bucket?

So, after seeing your health care professional and ruling out chemical imbalances, clinical depression and wonky hormones, begin choosing happiness today.

We have all heard the saying – Fake it till you make it.

Believe it or not, science has proven that if you smile when you don't feel like smiling; walk with your head up and a spring in your step; pretend to laugh and tell yourself you are a happy, joyful person, it does change your brain chemistry.

Your brain begins to release endorphins, melatonin and other lovely neurotransmitters associated with feeling great, having an optimistic outlook on life and getting a good night's sleep.

There have been many books written on the mind/body connection, not only by doctors but philosophers as well.

As you begin this journey to creating your own happiness, a good start may be reading at least one book about the value of being happy.

This way you can begin with a good understanding of, not only how this is possible to "fake it till you make it" from a medical standpoint, but why it is, literally, a matter of life and death to choose happiness.

This is not new research, by any means. The ancient Greeks understood the connection between mind and body very well.

Epicurus was a philosopher who lived 2300 years ago. He devoted his life to the study of happiness and how to achieve it.

Epicurus believed that the worst 'buzz kill' was fear of the future.

In this day and age it seems as though we have more things to fear than ever before.

We haven't quite achieved world peace, yet. We worry about global warming. We worry about job cutbacks. We worry about the weird, wild weather. We worry about the crazies out there that threaten our safety.

We live in challenging times. It is my belief that it is more important than ever to find as many ways as we can to create happiness in our lives and the lives of our fellow 'passengers' on this earthly trip.

Consider this: When faced with a challenge, are you able to think more clearly of a solution when you are scared witless and worried about every possible nasty outcome or when you are calm enough to see things from a new perspective?

When we are scared and worried, many of us become immobilized. We just can't think of what to do, where to turn or how things are ever going to be OK.

And although you may be in a situation where a Happy Dance is neither an option nor appropriate, the brain chemistry is radically altered when you shift your thinking to one of positive attitude.

Your fight or flight response that is telling you to just get the hell out of there or fight like you are in the UFC, is in control. You simply cannot think clearly.

Yet, if you shift your mind and brain to more positive thoughts, the chemicals simmer down and you can think more clearly.

This is the mind/body connection and one of the reasons it is so important to focus on those happy, positive emotions.

Dr. Deepak Chopra also writes about this connection on many levels. He has devoted a large part of his life to educating and helping people to attain and maintain a healthy, positive outlook.

Bernie Siegel, M.D. writes about his work with cancer patients using the mind/body connection to help them deal with fear, pain, drug reactions and more.

He found that by maintaining a higher degree of optimism and a happier outlook on life in general had a very positive effect physiologically.

His books are amazing.. We discovered them when our Mom had cancer and, for me, his insight helped so much.

Dr. Wayne Dyer and Louise Hay have also taught and written extensively on the power of our mind and how positive thoughts, affirmations and beliefs help us live healthier, happier lives.

It's not longer just WooWoo, folks! It's Science!

Throughout this book you will find many tips to help elevate your mood and shift you from sad to happy.

Here are a few ideas to get you started.

Giving to others in a way that makes you feel good. Volunteer at a shelter, as a coach, a Big Brother or Big Sister, your church, an event in your town.

Working with others towards a common goal creates real changes within your brain that promote happiness. We are, indeed, mysterious creatures.

Blowing bubbles outside. Yes, it is important to let your inner child out to play everyday and this is so much fun.

Listen to children laughing. A really good way to find children laughing is to simply enter the phrase into YouTube.

Boy, there are some funny babies and you can't stop yourself from laughing once you hear them. That laughter comes from a place that is pure joy.

You just can't help but start laughing along with them.

Watch a funny movie or TV show.

If you like British humor you might want to check out a TV series from BBC a few years back called Coupling.

It's like Friends on Viagra. No, it's not porn but *very* risqué. And so funny! My face hurt, my stomach hurt and we had to stop the DVD a few times so my husband could get up off the floor and stop crying.

Yeah, it's that good.

Art is a wonderful way to shift emotional states. Whether you change your state of being as the artist or as the viewer, the effect is profound.

We all have our ups and downs and one of my favorite mood shifters is the work of an artist named Kim Jacobs.

She creates the most beautiful calendars. Her work is pencil and layered water colors. The scenes she creates draw me in and it is as if I have been transported to another world.

Her work, called Cobblestone Way, is whimsical, colorful and full of calming scenes from the turn of the century.

Music is also a very powerful mood changer. You can use meditation and harmonics music, rock, indie, multicultural, classics from any era.

One word of caution, though; if you are listening to country music, make sure you choose songs where the beer is full, their dog is still alive and their wife/girlfriend/husband/boyfriend is still in the picture.

Read inspirational stories and books. Chicken Soup For The Soul is a great place to start. But don't just head to the adults section of the bookstore.

Children's books are some of the best mood changers, ever. They are written to evoke happy feelings. And the artwork can be simply magical.

Some of my favorites are

- Grandfather Twilight. The artwork is so beautiful and I love the simple story.
- Because a Small Bug Went Ka-Choo. This book is so much fun. Every child loves it. I can't tell you any more. I don't want to spoil it for you.
- Anything by Robert Munsch. His books are so fun
- and silly that you just have to laugh. Thomas' Snowsuit is hilarious and he has it down when it comes to trying to get a little wiggly kid into a snowsuit.
- Dr. Seuss. Of course!
- Jody Bergsma – Lovely artwork and stories
- If You Give A Mouse A Cookie.

Read a biography of someone who you admire. How have they overcome their struggles and found happiness in their lives? Let their lives inspire you to find your own road to happiness.

I know that not every day seems like a good day. We all have to face unhappy situations at some point in our lives. I have used all of these ideas at one time or another. At heart, though, I am a Pollyanna. I know there is a silver lining somewhere, even if I can't see it through all the crap.

I know that if we allow ourselves to remain in a state of unhappiness for too long, each day becomes a struggle. We, as human beings, can be faced with such terrible circumstances, yet we are the most incredible, resilient brave beings.

It is so important that we get back up, dust ourselves off and carry on. Our ability to do that and lift others up along the way is truly an inspiration.

Remember, when the pain of living is great and you just don't think you can get up one more time, there are many people out there who are willing and able to help.

There are ministers, doctors, help lines, community service organizations, friends, neighbors, bartenders, and sometimes even a stranger on the bus that are there to help.

Those who live with a spiritual belief take great comfort in their own idea of God, Creator, Source, the Universal Mind, the All That Is - whatever you choose to call that magic that we are a part of.

You are never alone! Ever!

Make this week *your* week to create happiness in your life. No one can do it for you and you really don't want anyone else to.

It is time for *you* to take charge of your life, your dreams, and your happiness. It's a way of telling yourself; "Self, I Love You."

Now smile, give yourself a hug and begin today.

Who do you have as your Happy Bucket Support Team?

Take the time to search out someone you can trust; friends, therapists, at your church, or local health center.

There are so many organizations that are able to provide, not only support, but the tools to take you from where you are to where you want to be: Happy and Empowered.

Time to do your Happy Dance.

Doing Your Happy Dance

List 5 things you can do to create a more
positive state of mind today?
Who is your support team?
List 3 things that make you happy today &
keep adding to your list.

Make Yourself
A Priority

Self Care
Is
Sexy As Hell

Make a Date with Yourself

"How beautiful it is to do nothing, and then to rest afterward."

Spanish Proverb

Make a date with yourself. Weird, right?

Or is it Genius?

Our lives are busier now than ever. We forget or feel as though we don't have time to slow down, to just do nothing, to do something that we enjoy that is just for us.

Is it any wonder that stress related dis-ease is a killer? So think of it this way.

Take a break as though your life depends on it. –

Making a date with yourself doesn't sound like such a crazy idea now, does it?

Here is a great idea designed to encourage you to schedule time for self-care.

An "enjoy your life" calendar where you actually schedule time for activities that are fun for you and will add to the quality and enjoyment of your life.

Grab a calendar with artwork that relaxes you, calms you, makes you laugh and recharges your spirit.

You could put anything down on this calendar, from taking time to lie in the sun for 10 minutes to taking a 2 week cruise where you are pampered from head to toe.

Start small with just 15 minutes or a half hour every other day to sit and read a favorite book, take a walk, play with your cat, dog, kids.

Try a short meditation, do your nails, listen to some favorite tunes, have fast, fun sex with your Sweetie or on your own, rest as though you are on vacation.

These little moments every day are just for you and are only limited by your imagination. Have fun with this.

Grab your calendar and start setting aside those small blocks of time that allow you to re-connect, relax, rejuvenate.

Make A Date With Yourself

What a wonderful gift to just take time for
you. Jot down some fun ideas then
take action!
What are some of your favorite things to do?
Dance? A cooking class? Wine tasting tour?
Make it fun!

Everything's
Gonna Be
OK

My Dad

Miss you, Dad.
xoxo

Gifts from my Dad

"He didn't tell me how to live; he lived, and let me watch him do it."
- Clarence Budington Kelland

There are many gifts my Dad gave me over the years. Some I learned during fun and pleasant times with him, some I received from the challenges of our earlier years. Each and every gift, though, is precious and I would not change one single thing about the way they were given.

My Dad wasn't always the most pleasant guy to be around when I was growing up. He drank a lot and was a miserable jerk. By dealing with him during my teen years, I can now argue black really is white. I could have been a lawyer.

He quit drinking in 1977, just a month before our first baby girl was born.   As he was sitting in the bar, drinking with his buddies, a friend who had join Alcoholics Anonymous sat down with them and said he would sponsor all of them.

Dad accepted the challenge, never took another drink and outlived all of them by at least 10 years. Even his sponsor went back to drinking eventually.

It wasn't easy. The relationship with my Mom was damaged beyond repair. I don't think she ever forgave him for the things he had put her through.

Dad joined every club and organization he could find. He knew that if he didn't keep busy, he would be drinking again.

At one point he was a member of at least 13 organizations and groups and gave tirelessly of his time and energy.

One of his greatest joys was helping with Special Olympics kids and taking them all on the bus to competitions in larger cities.

Dad loved planes and was one of the founding members of our local airshow. It started off small, just a fly-in and free pancake breakfast for those overnighters, many of whom slept under their planes for the night.

As the airshow grew to a huge 3-day event, he used his skills as a lineman for the power company to completely wire the sound and lighting systems.

After joining AA he found himself dedicating much of his time to becoming an AA sponsor. Many times he would receive phone calls in the middle of the night from someone who was teetering, ready to fall off the wagon. Dad would go and help them stay strong and get through the crisis.

Dad also helped co-found a society that would help create employment opportunities for single moms. He was instrumental, as well, in starting a program to educate the public about the dangers of alcohol to expectant mothers and their babies.

I learned the gift of generosity and giving from my Dad.

Dad had a great sense of humor. He loved all kinds of jokes including practical jokes, which he loved to play on his buddy, Mike.

He got Mike good when he created an "official" letter from National Geographic saying they would like to come and visit Mike's organic blueberry farm. Mike was pretty excited about this honor until he found out Dad was behind it.

Mike got him back pretty good later that summer when he caught Dad napping under his special tree. Mike snuck up and caught Dad on camera.

 He then put together a short video of a vulture, circling overhead as Dad slept on, the Good, the Bad and the Ugly theme playing in the background.

Dad said one of his favorite things to do was to simply sit back and watch my sisters and brother and I laugh our way through whatever life threw at us.

We used laughter to relieve the stress of our Mother's 30-day battle with pancreatic cancer.   Mom was in on many of the jokes. She has such a fun sense of humor and a great, hearty laugh so we used all sorts of tricks to get her laughing.

We cried, of course, and grieved deeply, but I'm grateful that those last days were also filled with laughter.

So from Dad I learned the gift of changing what I could when life threw me a curve ball and to do my best to laugh at the rest.

I loved visiting with my Dad.   He always had great stories to tell and I was touched by number of people that he still stayed in touch with.

He took the time to visit with friends he knew in grade school.   He would find out where a work buddy was from his early days as a lineman for the power company and give him a call.

He made friends easily and never forgot them.   He would always call me up and brag about having all of his 50 or so Christmas cards done and mailed by the first week of December.

These relationships from the various phases of life are important, I think. They certainly were to my Dad and he cherished them. They remind us of where we have come from, the people that helped take us to where we are now and the things we learned, along the way.

I learned the gift of being grateful for those I have shared life's path with and to reconnect with them whenever I can.

Dad was one of the oldest people to take up skydiving in our town. At 55 years old he strapped on his parachute for the first time. He made at least 30 jumps before he packed up his parachute for good.

But he wasn't done flying yet.

He learned to fly and bought his own floatplane so he could go fishing at some of the hard-to-get-to lakes in the area.

He loved to buzz our house, making one pass to let us know he was there, then coming around for a second pass so we could have the kids outside to wave at him. The silly bugger came in so low one time the kitchen floor shook and one of the kids dove under the bed.

He was the oldest person ever to bungee jump off one particular bridge in New Zealand. Our Mom and us kids were all incredibly grateful that he let us know about it *after* he had survived.

I learned from my Dad the gift of seeing life as an adventure and being unafraid to experience new things regardless of how old we are. Age never stopped him from doing much of anything.

Dad was always game for something silly.

One year some great family friends had a tacky tourist party at their farm in the Gulf Islands, off the coast of British Columbia. I have seen Dad in his work clothes, his gardening clothes and his dress clothes.

For our daughter's wedding I even got to see him in his full dress Scottish kilt, jacket and knee socks.

He and my brother looked amazing in their matching Smith tartans as they stepped up to help our daughter down from the carriage that brought her to the wedding site.

But I have never seen Dad in psychedelic flower shorts with his skinny, white, chicken legs sticking out. It was hilarious.

Then a few years ago, when a bunch of us high school girl friends turned 50, these wild and crazy friends threw a huge dress-up birthday bash on the farm. People from ages 5 to 85 came from far and near.

We had all the stars:

A lovely woman dressed as the Queen of England; RedGreen, the king of duct tape; 2 Clint Eastwoods from his spaghetti westerns; Cruella Deville; assorted hippies; a lovely fairy or two and even Captain Jack Sparrow.

It was a great party. But my favorite memory is sharing this time with my Dad.

Dad loved music. When we were little he signed us up for Columbia House Record Club. We grew up listening to some unusual and diverse music. One month might be Chubby Checker or Johnny Horton, the next would be Swiss yodeling , But he liked country and bluegrass the best.

So he chose the most unique person to become. He was dressed as an iconic Canadian musician named Stompin' Tom Connors, which was perfect because my Dad's name was Tom.

Stompin' Tom was famous for.......well, for his stomping. As he played his guitar and sang those great songs of Canada; the Snowmobile Song, the Hockey Song and Bud the Spud, his big, black cowboy boots would stomp the beat on a piece of plywood.

If he hadn't had that square of plywood, Stompin' Tom would have worn a hole in every stage floor he sang from.

So Dad dressed up in his best black cowboy shirt and jeans, found himself a big black cowboy hat, created his own guitar out of plywood and hung a piece of plywood around his neck for stompin'.

He became Stompin' Tom. He even wrote a song for the occasion.

So Stompin' Tom and his side-kick daughter, Janis Joplin (that's me) were a hit. What a great time we had.

Although my Dad passed away in 2009, his gifts to me will always help to guide me throughout my own life and I just want to say.

"Thanks Dad, you handsome devil."

You taught me the gift of not taking myself too seriously.

Don't be so afraid of looking silly that you miss out on all the fun of a life filled with moments that make the most precious memories.

This week take the time to look at those gifts.

What life lessons or gifts from your parents are you grateful for? No matter how hard and difficult your life with your parents may have been, there are gifts within that experience. Find them and honor them.

How do these gifts help you in your life today?

Are you aware of the gifts you can give your own children?

If your parents are still living, tell them how their life has been a gift to you.

Sometimes the gift is seeing how NOT to live your life. My Dad certainly gave us plenty of *those* gifts during his drinking years.

The greatest gift you can give yourself is to forgive them and show your children *your* best life.

Gifts From My Dad

What are some of the lessons,
both joyful and painful,
that your parents taught you?

EH,
Good Enough

Mediocrates

Well, you have come to the end of the book but the beginning of a new you.

I hope that as you read through the pages of **From Bitchy to Bitchin' – 13 Tips To Be Happy Now**, you were able to find ideas to shift your emotions that you can make your very own.

This little book gives you the power to see the world from a different perspective. Give yourself a chance to really enjoy life. Use as many of these tips as you feel like using in any order you wish to use them.

Add your own unique touch any of them. Tweak each one to make it your own. You have creative control.

When you change something, even in a small way, to make it your own, that is a wonderful way of honoring yourself. I would like you to recognize that. Give value to your desires and your uniqueness.

Look at these tips as a recipe for a casserole. It calls for certain ingredients and providing you have the basic "sauce to rice or noodle" ratio right you can get creative. Add tarragon or curry powder, throw in cashews or almonds, take out those mushrooms and add red and yellow peppers or jalapenos.

Yeah, I hate mushrooms and love peppers!

I wrote this book because I know it is not always easy to happy every day. The blues can hit from out of nowhere and you may even want to wallow in it for a time. But don't let it become a habit.

It is not a healthy state of being and life is too unpredictable to spend time hanging out in that black pit.

It is so important for you to know that you *can* change your state of mind and that you are worthy of living a life of happiness and joy.   Don't be fooled into thinking that only the big things like a new car, a trip or a truckload of money dumped in your front yard can make you happy.

Let the small things that you experience every day make you happy. It can be as simple as a child laughing or getting the perfect parking spot.

I love the sun on my face, hugs from my grandkids, the first leaves of spring after 6 months of winter and those incredible nights that show a zillion stars. It's all magic.

I love the big stuff, too. Traveling around the world, swimming with the dolphins in Kona, meditation in the King's Chamber of the Great Pyramid, white water rafting, having enough money to share with causes I believe in, a new vehicle and lying on a beach on some far off tropical island all make me very happy.

This book is not for everyone and that's perfect. Recognizing that it doesn't work for you is all part of living your life in a way that empowers you. It doesn't have a lot of scientific background, just a lot of life experience that I wanted to share.

It is important to remember that there are times when you DO need to see your health care or mental health care professional. It's OK to ask for help and being courageous enough to ask for help is another way of honoring yourself. It is not a sign of weakness but of great self-love.

Life is all about honoring yourself. What is your truth, what works for you, what makes you happy, what feeds your soul and makes you dance, even on the inside?

Bless you all on your journey.

Vicky M. Ford

Connect with me:

25
Homemade
Gifts For Christmas &
Special Occasions
Super Fast & Easy
Food Gifts
Vicky Ford

101 Ways
To De-Stress
Your Life
Vicky M. Ford

My
Cabin Fever
Batshit Crazy
F*CK YOU, VIRUS
Self Reflection
Journal
It's Fine. I'm Fine.
Everything's Fine.

25 Words That
Can Change
Your Life
The Power To Be Amazing
Lies Within You
Vicky Ford

Bliss Me Out
Coloring Book
- Calm -
50 Coloring Mandalas to Calm & Relax

Bliss Me Out
Coloring Book
- Beauty -
50 Coloring Mandalas Bringing Beauty
To Your Life

SHIT I SAY
WHEN I'M
DRUNK

My
Healing
Journey
60 Day Journal
Vicky Ford
Dancing Tree Publishing

What If...
100
Weird Ass Things
To
Ponder

A 90-Day Journal
Soul's Journey
- Healing -
Vicky M. Ford

www.ingramcontent.com/pod-product-compliance
Lightning Source LLC
Chambersburg PA
CBHW051545050726
47595CB00002B/648